The Cup in the Forest

Anne Collins

T0351243

Easystart

Series Editors: Andy Hopkins and Jocelyn Potter

1.1 What's the book about?

1 Look at the pictures in this book. What country is this story about?

   a China   **b** Egypt   **c** Australia   **d** Norway

2 What is the story about? What do you think?

   a love   **b** animals   **c** a family   **d** a ghost

3 Look at pictures A and B. Talk about them with a friend. Then write answers.

A Why is this important in the story?

....

....

....

B Why is he important in the story?

....

....

....

1.2 What happens first?

Look at the words at the bottom of pages 1–3. What are they in your language? Then look at the pictures on the same pages. Put the right words in the sentences.

1 The boy and the girl are in a .... | school   forest   town |

2 They are .... | swimming   driving   walking |

3 There are many .... | trees   people   animals |

4 The forest is very .... | beautiful   dark   small |

5 They find a .... | bottle   knife   cup |

Per and his girlfriend, Nina, live in a big town in Norway. They are on holiday in the country. They are driving on a road near a big **forest**.

'It's beautiful here,' Per says. 'Let's stop the car and walk in the forest.'

But the forest is very dark and quiet. 'I don't like this place,' Nina says. 'I'm cold. Let's go back to the car.'

Suddenly, Per falls **over** a tree.

forest /ˈfɒrəst/ (n) I love trees. I walk in the *forest* every evening after work.
over /ˈəʊvə/ (prep) The road goes *over* the river and then into town.

'Are you OK?' Nina asks.

'Yes,' Per answers. Then he sees some old **stone**s. 'These are very **strange** stones,' he says. He moves them with his hands. They are very heavy. 'There's a **hole** under the stones,' he says. He puts his hand into the hole.

'Be **careful**,' Nina says. 'Perhaps an animal lives in there.'

Per takes his hand from the hole. He has an old **cup** in his hand.

stone /stəʊn/ (n) He is building a house with the *stones*, but they are very heavy.
strange /streɪndʒ/ (adj) Her brother has black hair, but her hair is red. That's *strange*.
hole /həʊl/ (n) There is a *hole* in my shoe and water is coming in.
careful /ˈkeəfəl/ (adj) Be *careful* on the road. There are no street lights.
cup /kʌp/ (n) Do you want a *cup* of coffee?

'Look at this old cup, Nina!' he says. 'It's very interesting. But why is it here? And look! There are some strange **word**s on it.'

Nina looks at the cup too. 'It's beautiful,' she says. She looks again. 'And very expensive!' she thinks.

word /wɜːd/ (n) We can't understand the *words* on this bottle. Are they Spanish or Italian?

The forest is very dark and cold.
'Let's go now,' Nina says. 'I don't like this forest.'
They walk back to their car. Suddenly, Per stops.
'What is it?' Nina asks.
Per looks into the trees. 'There's a man there,' he says.
Nina looks too. 'I can't see a man,' she says.
Per looks again. 'You're right,' he says. 'It's only a tree.'

Per and Nina drive to a small town.

'It's getting dark,' Per says. 'Let's stay in this town.'

They find a small hotel. The people are very friendly.

'I like this hotel,' Nina says. 'Let's stay here.'

Near the hotel is a **museum**.

'We can take the cup to the museum in the morning,' Per says. 'We can ask the **curator** about it.'

museum /mjuːˈziəm/ (n) You can see very old photographs in the town's *museum*.
curator /kjʊˈreɪtə/ (n) Is this old Roman money? Let's ask the *curator*.

2.1 Were you right?

Look at your answers to Activity 1.2. Are your answers right?

1 What is first? And then? Write the numbers, 1–4.

2 Write the right sentences under the pictures.

- Per and Nina look at the cup.   • Per moves the stones with his hands.
- Per and Nina go for a walk in the forest.   • Per and Nina drive to the town.

2.2 What more did you learn?

Put the words in the box in the right places.

| museum   forest   strange   hotel   cup   words   stones |

Per and Nina are walking in a ¹................................ . Per sees some
old ²............................... . He moves them and finds an old
³............................... . There are some ⁴............................... on it. They
are very ⁵............................... . Then Per and Nina drive to a
⁶............................... . There is a ⁷............................... near the hotel.

2.3 Language in use

Look at the sentence on the right. Then write *a*, *an*, *the* or *some* in the sentences.

> 'There's **a** hole under **the** stones.'

Per puts his hand into ¹............... hole. 'Perhaps there's ²...............
animal there,' Nina says. Per finds ³............... old cup in ⁴...............
hole. There are ⁵............... strange words on it. Nina looks at
⁶............... cup too. 'That's ⁷............... very beautiful cup,' she thinks.
'And very expensive!'

2.4 What happens next?

Look at the words at the bottom of pages 8–13. Then look at the pictures on this page. What are the people thinking? What do you think? Write the letters, a–d.

a 'That cup belongs to me.'

b 'I can sell the cup and get some money.'

c 'Take the cup back to the forest.'

d 'I'm afraid of the strange man.'

Later, Per can't sleep. He goes to the window of his room and looks into the hotel garden.

A strange man is standing there. He doesn't move.

'Who are you?' Per **call**s. 'What do you want?'

Then Nina comes into the room.

'There's a strange man in the garden,' Per says.

'What man?' Nina asks. 'I can't see a man.'

call /kɔːl/ (v) Listen! The teacher *is calling* your name.

In the morning, Per and Nina take the cup to the museum. The museum curator is an old man.

'Do you know about this cup?' Per asks.

The curator looks at the cup for a long time. 'Where is it from?' he asks.

'From a hole under some old stones in the forest,' Per says.

'Take the cup back to the forest . . . now,' the curator says.

'But why?' Per asks.

'Do you see the old words on the cup?' the curator asks.

'They say *This cup **belong**s to Hakon. Be careful!*'

'Who is Hakon?' Per asks.

'Hakon is an old Viking* name,' the curator says. 'There are some Viking **grave**s in the forest. This cup is from Hakon's grave. Take it back there ... now!'

---

* Viking: a name for Scandinavian people from about the years 790–1066

belong /bɪˈlɒŋ/ (v) Does this coat *belong* to you?
grave /greɪv/ (n) This is my mother's *grave*: 'Lisa Brown 1946–2008'.

Per and Nina are drinking coffee in the hotel.

'Let's take the cup back to the forest,' Per says.

'Are you **crazy**?' Nina says. 'Why do you listen to the old man's stories? Hakon is only a dead Viking.'

'Yes,' Per says. 'But I'm **afraid**. The cup belongs to him.'

Suddenly, Per sees the strange man across the room. 'Look!' he says. 'Hakon is here! He's in this café!'

crazy /ˈkreɪzi/ (adj) He is *crazy*. He dances all night in his garden.
afraid /əˈfreɪd/ (adj) I am *afraid* of big animals – and very small animals!

11

Per runs across the room. But Hakon isn't there.

Then Per goes back to the table. But Nina isn't there! And the bag with the cup isn't there!

He runs to the door of the hotel. He sees Nina in the car. She is driving away from the hotel very **fast**.

'Stop, Nina!' Per calls. 'Where are you going?'

But Nina doesn't stop. She is driving away with the cup.

fast /fɑːst/ (adv) People drive very *fast* down this street.

Nina drives away from the town. She is driving fast, very fast. But she isn't afraid. She is thinking about money. Money is important to Nina.

The cup is in a bag near her. Nina looks at it and smiles. 'Per is crazy,' she thinks. 'He's afraid of old stories about dead Vikings. But the cup belongs to me now. I'm taking it to Oslo. I can **sell** it there.'

sell /sel/ (v) He *is selling* his old car. He wants a new car.

3.1 Were you right?

Look at your answers to Activity 2.4. Are your answers right? Then finish these sentences with the words on the right.

1 Per sees a strange man	about Hakon.
2 Per and Nina take the cup	from the town.
3 The curator talks to them	about money.
4 Hakon is	in Nina's bag.
5 Per and Nina drink coffee	in the garden.
6 Nina drives away	to the museum.
7 The cup is	in the hotel.
8 Nina is thinking	an old Viking name.

3.2 What more did you learn?

What can you see in the four pictures? Write the words under them. Then put the numbers of the pictures with the sentences.

....

a This belongs to Hakon.

b Hakon is one.

c This is in the forest.

d Nina puts the cup in this.

3.3 Language in use

Look at the sentence on the right. Then look at the pictures and finish the sentences. What are the people doing?

> A strange man **is standing** there.

1 The curator .... the cup.

2 Per and Nina .... coffee.

3 Nina .... the car fast.

4 Nina ....
.... money.

3.4 What happens next?

How does the story finish? What do you think? Look at the pictures on pages 16–19.

1 Nina takes the cup to Oslo.   Yes / No

2 She sells the cup.   Yes / No

3 The car falls into the river.   Yes / No

4 Hakon has his cup.   Yes / No

Per runs to the museum and finds the old curator.

'Where's the cup?' the curator asks.

'My girlfriend has it now,' Per answers.

'That's bad,' the curator says. 'The cup belongs to Hakon.'

'But Hakon is dead,' Per says.

'Yes,' the curator says, 'but there are strange stories about Viking **ghost**s. Take my car and go after your girlfriend!'

ghost /gəʊst/ (n) Sometimes, at night, I see a *ghost* in my room!

Nina drives for a long time. It is getting dark. There are no cars on the road. She can't see any towns or houses or people. Only forests. Dark, black forests. But Nina thinks about money again and she is happy.

Now it is raining. Suddenly, Nina sees a strange man. He is standing on the road. He is looking at Nina. His face is dark and angry.

Nina **scream**s and screams. She is very afraid. She can't stop the car and she can't see the road. She only sees the man's angry face. His eyes are cold and strange. They are the eyes of a dead man.

The car **leave**s the road and hits a tree. Then it falls into a river. The water closes over the car. It is very quiet. The car, Nina and the cup are in the river.

scream /skriːm/ (v) Why *is* that child *screaming*? Is he ill?
leave /liːv/ (v) I am *leaving* work now and I am going home.

18

Later, the police come and take the car from the river. A
policeman looks into the car.

'There's a girl in here,' he says. 'She's dead.'

Per is there too. He is very unhappy about Nina. Suddenly, he sees
a man. The man is walking into the forest.

'The ghost of Hakon!' Per thinks. He is very afraid. But Hakon is
walking away now. He has his cup.

Look at the picture and work with a friend.

1 What can you see in the picture?
2 What do Per and the policeman say?

Student A You are the policeman. Ask Per questions about Nina. Start: *Do you know this girl?*

Student B You are Per. Answer the policeman's questions.

Write about it

The curator is writing about Viking graves for visitors to the museum. Put these words in the right places.

| careful | ghosts | strange | forests | graves | belong |

Viking Graves

There are many beautiful green _____ near our town. You can find old Viking _____ in some of them. But be _____! Leave things in the graves. They _____ to the dead Vikings. There are many _____ stories about Viking _____.

> Work with one or two friends. You are famous writers of ghost stories. You are writing a new story.

1 **Talk to the curator at the museum. Ask questions.**

> Is/Are ...?   What ...?   Who ...?   Why ...?
> How ...?   When ...?   Where ...?

Yes, there is one.

Are there any ghosts near here?

2 **Where is the grave? Write the words in the sentences. Then put the places and things in the right places.**

> forest   cup   road   river   stones   grave   town   trees

a Go away from the ....

b Take the .... to the forest.

c Go over the ....

d Walk into the ....

e Look for the .... under the ....

f Hakon's .... is under the stones.

g But the .... stays there!

1 _____

2 _____

3 _____

4 _____

5 _____

6 _____

7 _____

8 _____

3 Talk to your friends and write sentences with the words in the box. Write about the forest, the cup and the ghost.

dark	cold	quiet	many trees	old	interesting	beautiful
	strange words	Viking man	long hair	angry face		

▶ The forest

....

....

....

▶ The cup

....

....

....

▶ The ghost

....

....

....

4 Now write your story.

Ghost of a Dead Viking

I am walking through a forest. The forest is ....

....

I see some stones under a tree. There is a hole under the stones. I put my hand in the hole. I take out a cup. It is very ....

....

But suddenly I see a man. He is ....

.... He is watching me. What does he want? I am very afraid!